PAUL ROBESON

The
Journey
of a
Renaissance
Man

Pomegranate

SAN FRANCISCO

Pomegranate Communications, Inc.
Box 6099, Rohnert Park, California 94927
800-227-1428
www.pomegranate.com

Pomegranate Europe Ltd.
Unit 1, Heathcote Business Centre, Hurlbutt Road
Warwick, Warwickshire CV34 6TD, U. K.

ISBN 0-7649-2383-8
Pomegranate Catalog No. AA196

Pomegranate publishes books of
postcards on a wide range of subjects.
Please contact the publisher for more information.

Cover designed by Shannon Lemme
Printed in China
11 10 09 08 07 06 05 04 03   10 9 8 7 6 5 4 3 2 1

To facilitate detachment of the postcards from this book, fold each card along its perforation line before tearing.

The photographs from the Robeson family collection that are reproduced here chronicle the highlights of Paul Robeson's fabulous career, from his days as honor student and All-American football star at Rutgers College through four decades of artistic triumphs as an actor and singer.

Paul Robeson was an original. He had no counterpart. He was a free spirit who came and went, belonging to multitudes but owned by no one. Like the wind rustling through a forest, or the moonlight shimmering on the surface of a still lake, he would not be confined.

My father's extraordinary journey through life was an odyssey that left indelible memories in the minds and hearts of the multitudes who were personally touched by his passage. He was not only a great artist but also one of the forerunners of the modern civil rights movement. As one of the most powerful black male images in American history, he made an enormous impact on our popular culture and undermined a myriad of antiblack stereotypes.

He became a great artist with a prophetic quality and a sense of divine mission. It is this inner spiritual commitment that shaped his character. The arc of his life and growth sweeps wider than that of most of our country's public figures, and the majesty of his achievements on the concert stage, in the theater, and in film sets him apart from most of his contemporaries.

By 1939, Paul Robeson, in his mature prime at forty-one, had joined Fyodor Chaliapin and Enrico Caruso as a member of a triumvirate of vocal artists who were in a class by themselves. Of these three, Robeson was the only one who achieved his recognition as a folk singer rather than as an opera singer.

His 1943–1944 Broadway performance in the title role of Shakespeare's *Othello* was hailed as the definitive performance in the modern history of the theater.

He was the first black leading man to star in nonstereotypical roles. Four of his eleven films, which were made in England and the United States, centered on African themes because he wanted his audiences to value African culture.

During World War II, he emerged as a unifying national symbol with his rendition of "Ballad for Americans," becoming the voice of democracy. But as the Cold War began, his continuing challenge to American racism and his friendship with Russia placed him in direct confrontation with the U.S. government. Under intensive government harassment throughout the 1950s, his passport was canceled, and he was blacklisted as a performing artist.

Despite this persecution, Paul Robeson remained committed to his principles. He died in retirement on January 23, 1976, at the age of seventy-seven. The late James Baldwin wrote that Paul Robeson gave people "the power to perceive and the courage to resist." The images you will encounter here are a window to that spiritual grace, which was an integral part of his personality.

—Paul Robeson, Jr.

PAUL ROBESON ▪ The Journey of a Renaissance Man

Paul Robeson, football All-American at Rutgers College, 1917. At 6'3"
and 220 pounds, Robeson was strong, fast, agile, and quick thinking.
One of the greatest ends of all time, he was a dominant college football player in 1917 and 1918.

BOX 6099   ROHNERT PARK   CA 94927

Pomegranate

PAUL ROBESON ▪ The Journey of a Renaissance Man

Paul Robeson, catcher on the Rutgers College varsity baseball team, 1919.

BOX 6099   ROHNERT PARK   CA 94927

Pomegranate

PAUL ROBESON • The Journey of a Renaissance Man

Paul Robeson's graduation photograph, Rutgers College, 1919. Robeson was chosen valedictorian of his graduating class.

BOX 6099   ROHNERT PARK   CA 94927

Pomegranate

PAUL ROBESON • The Journey of a Renaissance Man

Paul Robeson as a star professional football player for the Akron Pros, 1920. To pay his way through Columbia Law School, Robeson played three seasons of professional football—two with Akron and one with Milwaukee.

BOX 6099   ROHNERT PARK   CA 94927

Pomegranate

PAUL ROBESON ▪ The Journey of a Renaissance Man

Paul Robeson, portrait, London, 1925.

BOX 6099   ROHNERT PARK   CA 94927

Pomegranate

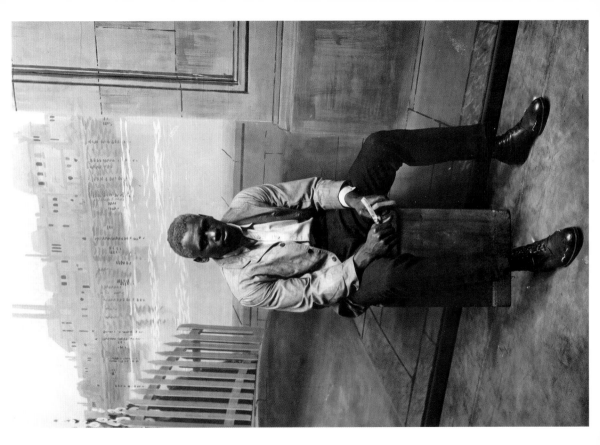

PAUL ROBESON ▪ The Journey of a Renaissance Man

Paul Robeson, thirty years old, performing the part of "Joe" in the musical *Show Boat* at Drury Lane Theatre, London, 1928.

BOX 6099   ROHNERT PARK   CA 94927

Pomegranate

PAUL ROBESON ▪ The Journey of a Renaissance Man

Paul Robeson publicity photograph, c. 1929. (Note the gold Phi Beta
Kappa key and gold basketball on the key chain.)

BOX 6099   ROHNERT PARK   CA 94927

Pomegranate

PAUL ROBESON ▪ The Journey of a Renaissance Man

Paul Robeson with his wife, Eslanda Cardozo Goode, London, 1930.

BOX 6099   ROHNERT PARK   CA 94927

Pomegranate

PAUL ROBESON • The Journey of a Renaissance Man

Paul Robeson in the title role of *Othello,* with Peggy Ashcroft as
Desdemona, Savoy Theatre, London, 1930. Othello: "It gives me wonder
great as my content to see you here before me." (Act 2, Scene i)

BOX 6099   ROHNERT PARK   CA 94927

Pomegranate

PAUL ROBESON ▪ The Journey of a Renaissance Man

Paul Robeson in a publicity pose, London, 1931.

BOX 6099   ROHNERT PARK   CA 94927

Pomegranate

PAUL ROBESON • The Journey of a Renaissance Man

Paul Robeson as "Jim," the lead role in Eugene O'Neill's play *All God's Chillun Got Wings,* Embassy Theatre, London, 1933.

BOX 6099   ROHNERT PARK   CA 94927

Pomegranate

PAUL ROBESON ▪ The Journey of a Renaissance Man

Paul Robeson in the title role of the film *The Emperor Jones,* New York, 1933. This was Robeson's first commercial film. Based on Eugene O'Neill's play, it was produced independently and launched Robeson's film career.

BOX 6099   ROHNERT PARK   CA 94927

Pomegranate

PAUL ROBESON ▪ The Journey of a Renaissance Man

Paul Robeson in the title role of the film *The Emperor Jones*, New York, 1933.

BOX 6099   ROHNERT PARK   CA 94927

Pomegranate

PAUL ROBESON ▪ The Journey of a Renaissance Man

Paul Robeson in the lead role of the film *Sanders of the River*, London, 1934. Despite its glorification of British colonialism, this film was the vehicle that catapulted Robeson to international film stardom.

BOX 6099   ROHNERT PARK   CA 94927

Pomegranate

PAUL ROBESON ▪ The Journey of a Renaissance Man

Paul Robeson in the lead role of the play *Stevedore,* Embassy Theatre,
London, 1935.

BOX 6099   ROHNERT PARK   CA 94927

Pomegranate

PAUL ROBESON ▪ The Journey of a Renaissance Man

Paul Robeson with costar Elisabeth Welch in the film *Song of Freedom,* London, 1936.

BOX 6099   ROHNERT PARK   CA 94927

Pomegranate

PAUL ROBESON ▪ The Journey of a Renaissance Man

Paul Robeson with costar Cedric Hardwicke (right) in the film *King Solomon's Mines,* London, 1936.

Pomegranate

BOX 6099　ROHNERT PARK　CA 94927

PAUL ROBESON ▪ The Journey of a Renaissance Man

Paul Robeson starring in the film *Big Fella,* with his wife, Eslanda, in a cameo role, London, 1937.

Pomegranate

BOX 6099   ROHNERT PARK   CA 94927

PAUL ROBESON ▪ The Journey of a Renaissance Man

Paul Robeson with costar Princess Kouka of the Sudan in the film
Jericho, Cairo, 1937.

BOX 6099   ROHNERT PARK   CA 94927

Pomegranate

PAUL ROBESON ▪ The Journey of a Renaissance Man

Paul Robeson with his only child, Paul, Jr., at a children's summer
camp, Folkstone, England, 1938.

BOX 6099   ROHNERT PARK   CA 94927

Pomegranate

PAUL ROBESON ▪ The Journey of a Renaissance Man

Paul Robeson starring in the film *Proud Valley*, Wales, 1939. Robeson plays the role of an unemployed black stoker who finds work in a Welsh coal mine. Filmed in the Rhondda mining valley with actual coal miners and their families, this was one of Robeson's two favorite films.

BOX 6099 ROHNERT PARK CA 94927

Pomegranate

PAUL ROBESON ▪ The Journey of a Renaissance Man

Paul Robeson at the podium during a civil rights rally, New York City, 1940.

BOX 6099   ROHNERT PARK   CA 94927

Pomegranate

PAUL ROBESON ▪ The Journey of a Renaissance Man

Paul Robeson in the title role of the musical *John Henry,* 44th Street
Theater, New York City, 1940.

BOX 6099   ROHNERT PARK   CA 94927

Pomegranate

PAUL ROBESON ▪ The Journey of a Renaissance Man

Paul Robeson in the title role of *Othello,* Shubert Theater, New York City, 1943. Othello: "It is the cause, it is the cause, my soul." (Act 5, Scene ii)

BOX 6099   ROHNERT PARK   CA 94927

Pomegranate

PAUL ROBESON • The Journey of a Renaissance Man

Paul Robeson speaking at a civil rights rally, New York City, 1949.

Pomegranate

BOX 6099 ROHNERT PARK CA 94927

PAUL ROBESON ▪ The Journey of a Renaissance Man

Paul Robeson being carried on the shoulders of students in Prague,
Czechoslovakia, during a 1949 visit.

BOX 6099   ROHNERT PARK   CA 94927

Pomegranate

PAUL ROBESON • The Journey of a Renaissance Man

Paul Robeson at the podium celebrating the 150th anniversary of
Alexander Pushkin's birth, Moscow, 1949. Robeson, an admirer of the
legendary African-Russian poet, delivered a speech in fluent Russian.

BOX 6099 ROHNERT PARK CA 94927

Pomegranate

PAUL ROBESON ▪ The Journey of a Renaissance Man

Paul Robeson announcing the song "Ol' Man River" at a concert in Moscow, 1949.

BOX 6099   ROHNERT PARK   CA 94927

Pomegranate

PAUL ROBESON ▪ The Journey of a Renaissance Man

Paul Robeson singing "My Curly-Headed Baby" at a concert in a
Harlem church, New York City, 1950. By 1950, Robeson was blacklisted
and could sing only in black churches or in left-wing union halls.

BOX 6099   ROHNERT PARK   CA 94927

Pomegranate

Paul Robeson in the Crimea, southern Russia, visiting a children's summer camp, 1958.

BOX 6099 ROHNERT PARK CA 94927

Pomegranate